ID0396633

This little book belongs to

_____

LIKE MOTHER, LIKE DAUGHTER

Written and Illustrated by Cathy Guisewite

Andrews and McMeel
A Universal Press Syndicate Company
Kansas City

ISBN: 0-8362-3049-3

LIKE MOTHER,
LIKE DAUGHTER

A daughter may
leave the nest, but she
never strays far
from the flock.

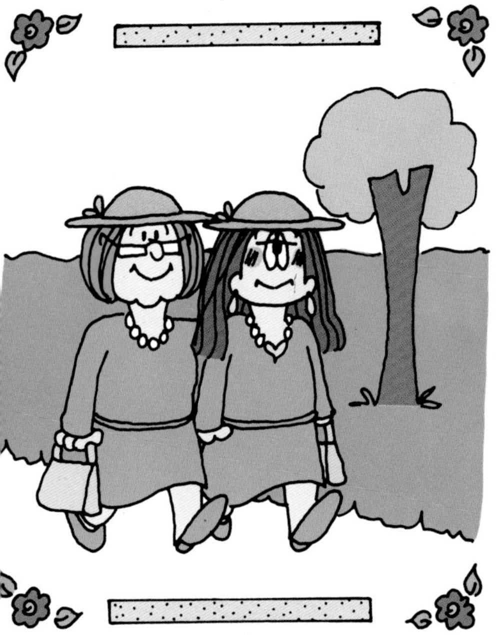

Even when a
mother knows she'll hate
her for it, it makes her
feel good to see her
daughter eat.

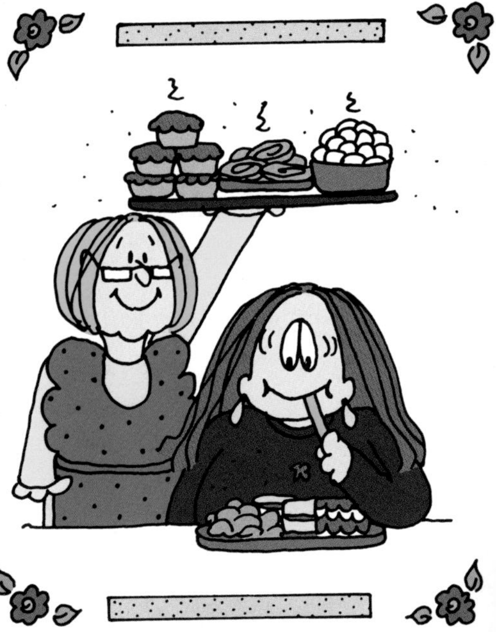

There's nothing
like a good fight to keep
a mother and daughter
speaking to each
other every day.

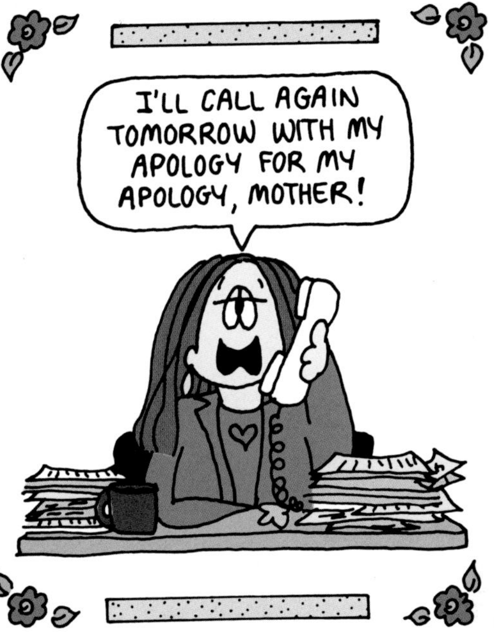
I'LL CALL AGAIN TOMORROW WITH MY APOLOGY FOR MY APOLOGY, MOTHER!

They'll turn away a
mother full of advice,
but no one ever says no
to one holding a mop.

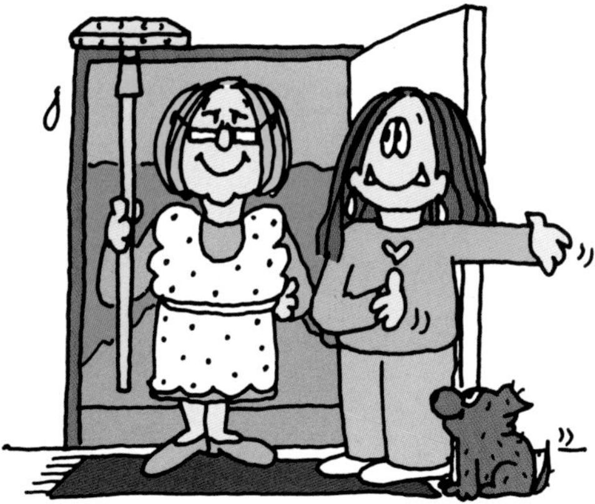

Mothers never sleep.
They just worry lying
down with their
eyes shut.

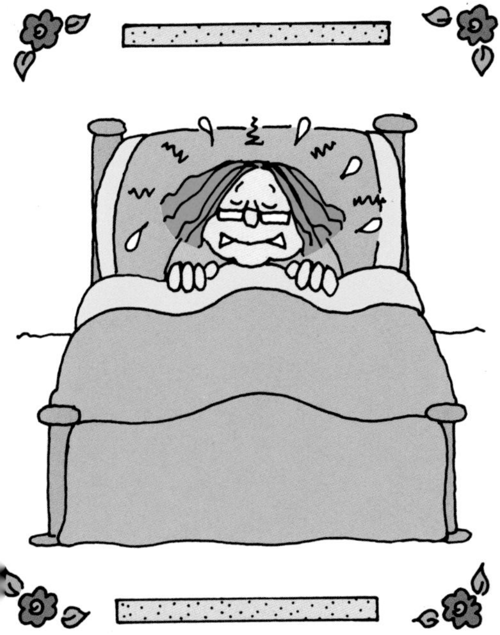

When a mother
finally has time to record
things in the baby book,
there's never anything
to report.

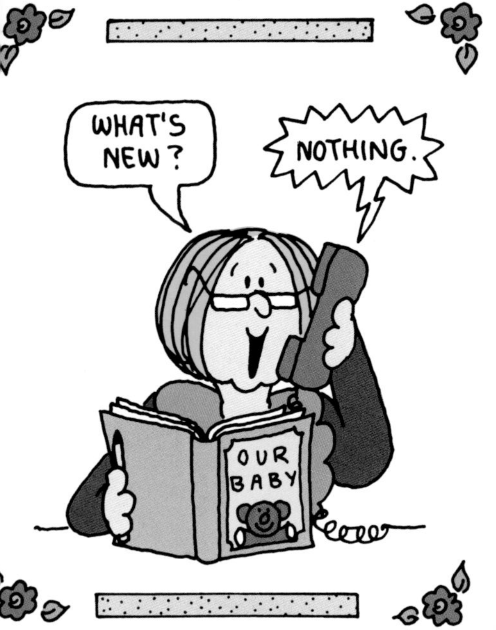
WHAT'S NEW?
NOTHING.
OUR BABY

The beauty of
following in a mother's
footsteps is that
they always lead
to the mall.

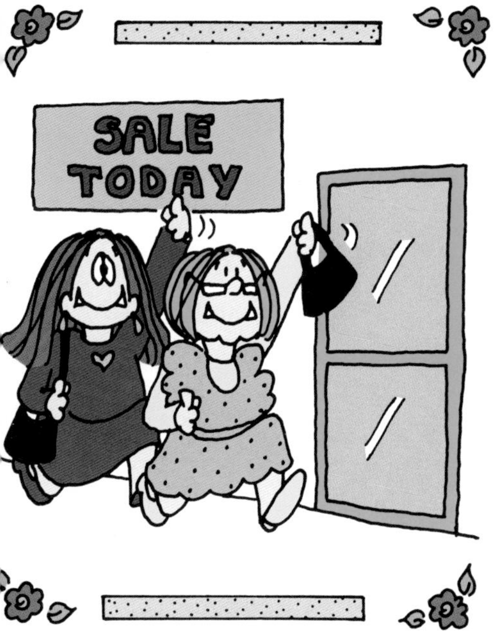
SALE
TODAY

Once a mother
has experienced the
thrill of creation,
it's hard to know
when to quit.

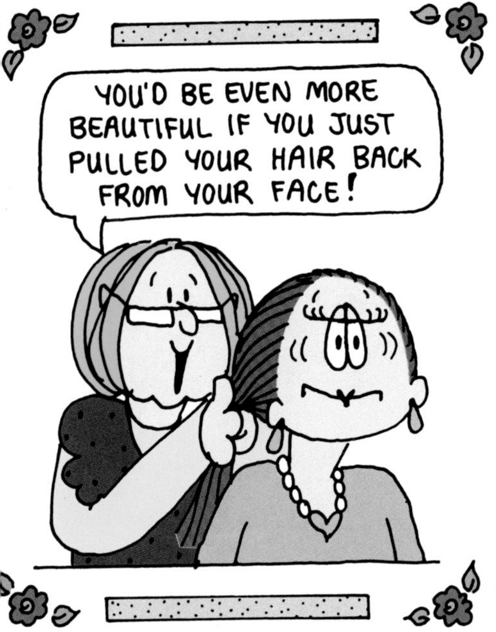
YOU'D BE EVEN MORE BEAUTIFUL IF YOU JUST PULLED YOUR HAIR BACK FROM YOUR FACE!

All mothers have
intuition. The great
ones have radar.

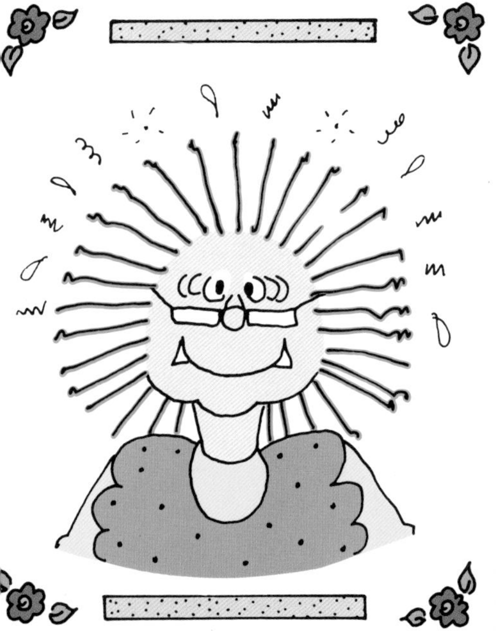

The story of a
mother's life:
Trapped between a
scream and a hug.

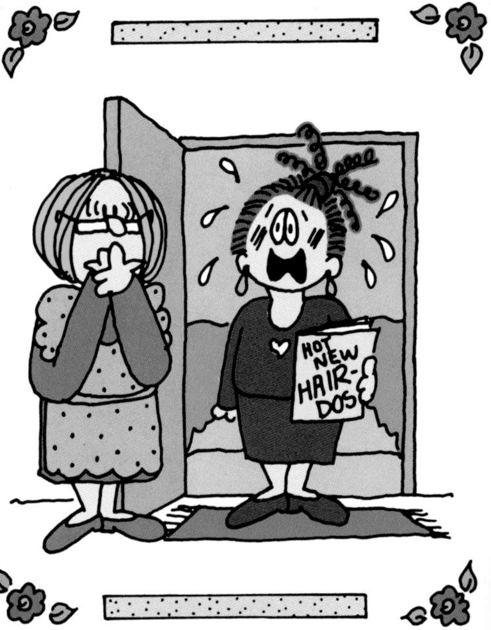
HOT NEW HAIR-DOS

There's a point
in every woman's life
where she not only
becomes her mother,
she surpasses her.

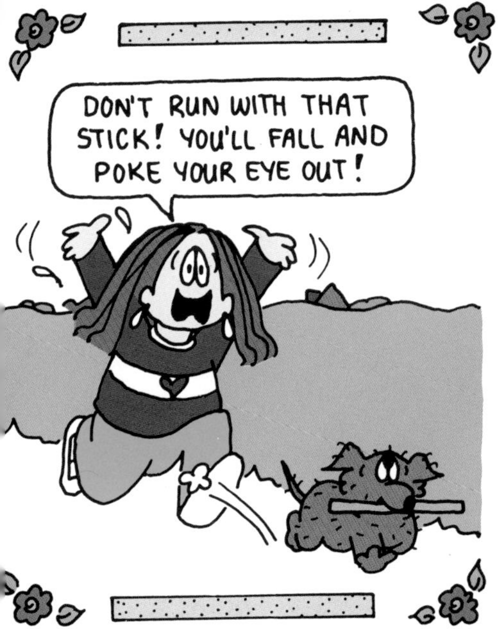
DON'T RUN WITH THAT STICK! YOU'LL FALL AND POKE YOUR EYE OUT!

Individually,
a mother and daughter
are scraps. Together,
they're a whole
newspaper.

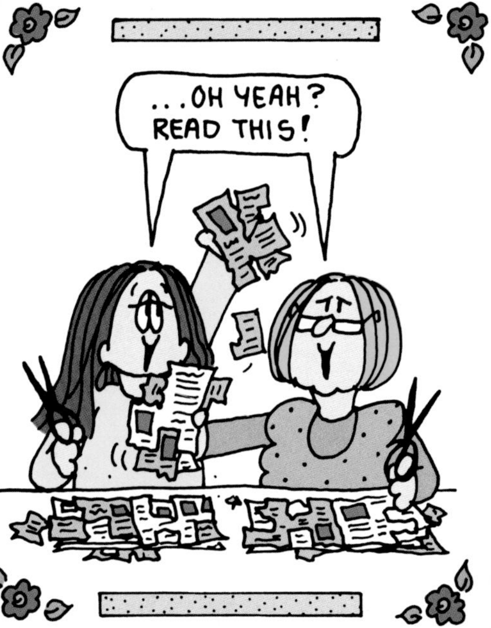
...OH YEAH? READ THIS!

A mother's prayer:
May her cup runneth
over, and may she
remember to putteth
a coaster under it
so it doesn't leaveth
a ring.

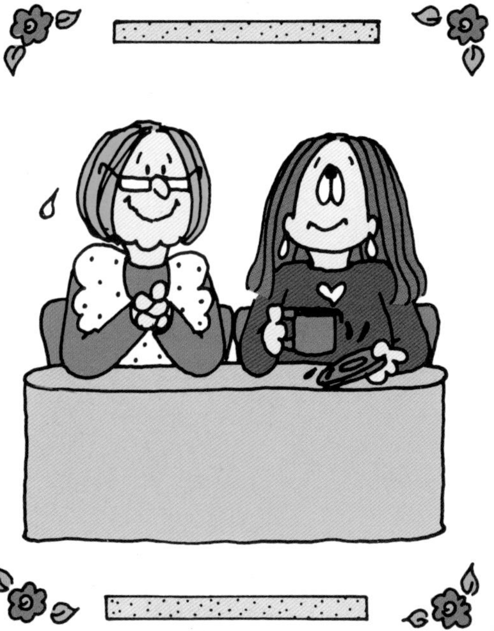

If necessity is the
mother of invention,
desperation is the
grandma.

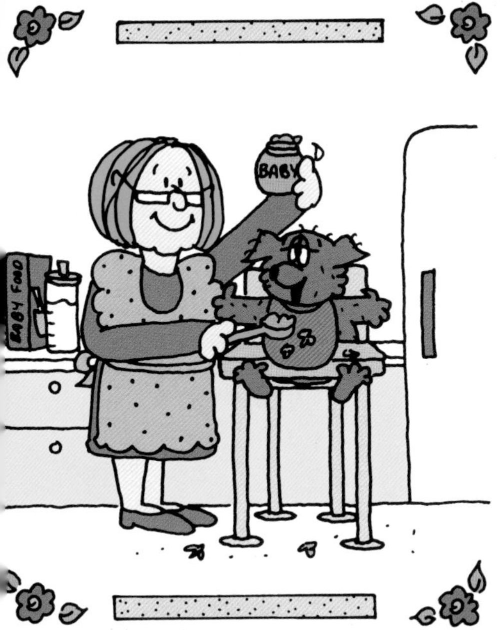
BABY
BABY FOOD

What a mother
doesn't know for sure,
she can make happen
anyway.

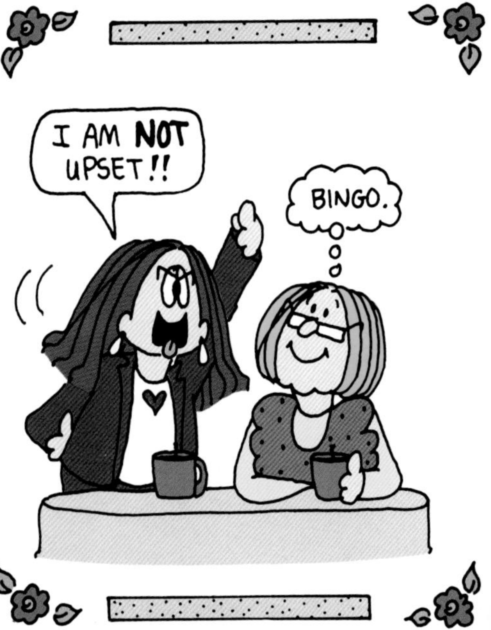
I AM NOT UPSET!!
BINGO.

A mother and
daughter find their
common ground, and
it's in front of the
return desk.

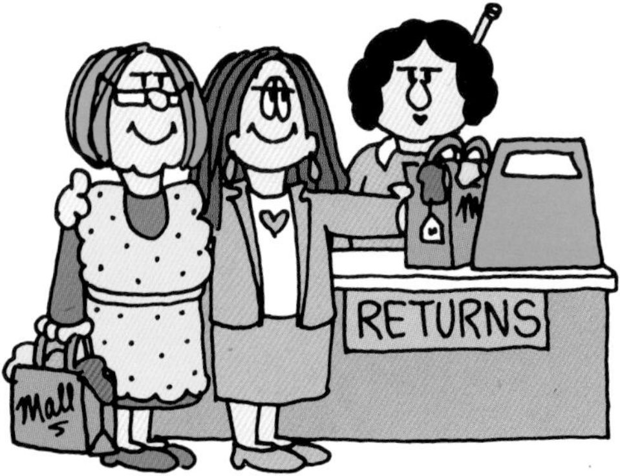
RETURNS
Mall

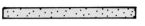

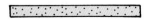

It takes a mother
to turn a few pearls
of wisdom into
a choker.

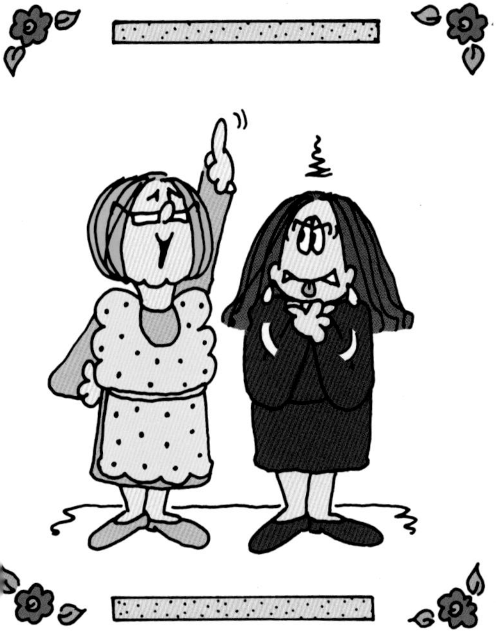

M.O.M.*

*Manager of Other people's Messes

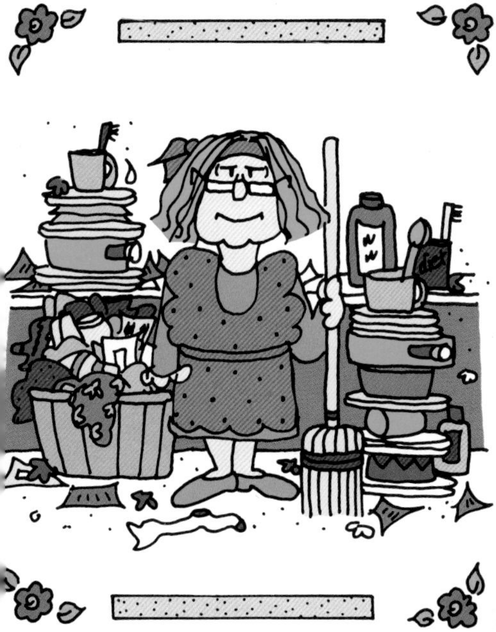

Nothing fills a mother
like a 15-phone-call
chicken dinner.

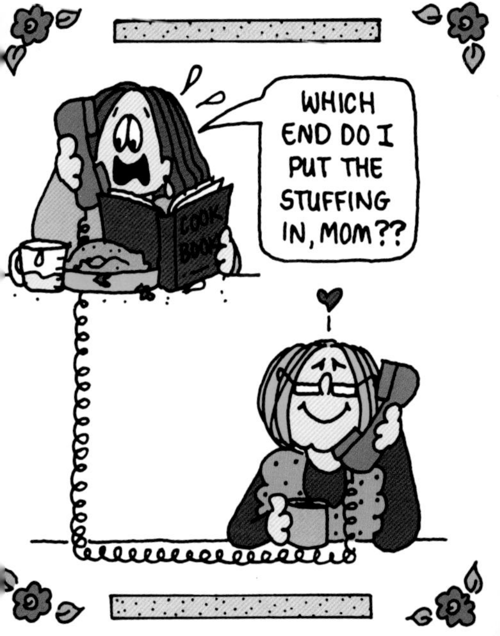
WHICH END DO I PUT THE STUFFING IN, MOM??
COOK BOOK

Even when she
knows she's the nerd,
a mother loves feeling
she's part of the group.

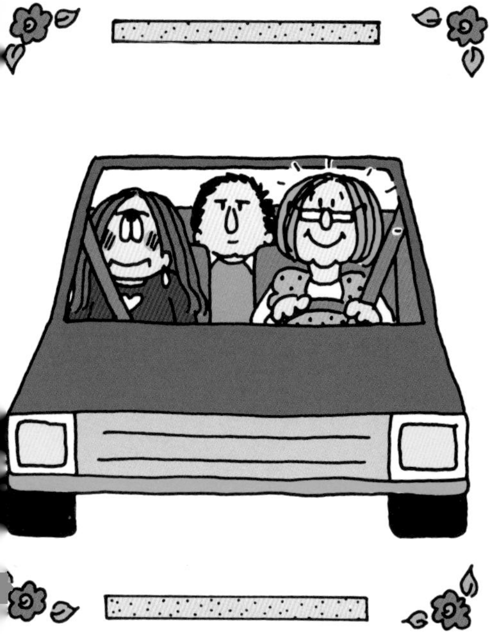

The only time a
mother knows for sure
her daughter's listening is
when she's no longer
speaking to her.

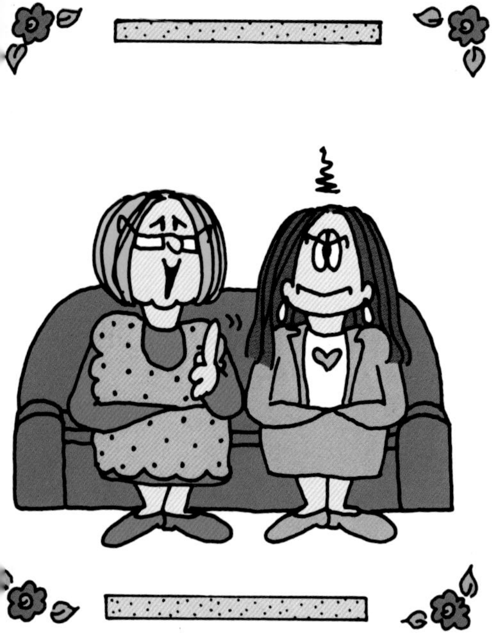

They may cut the
umbilical cord, but no
one will ever cut the
phone cord.

Mothers learn to
keep their mouths
closed. It keeps
"I told you so"
from jumping out.

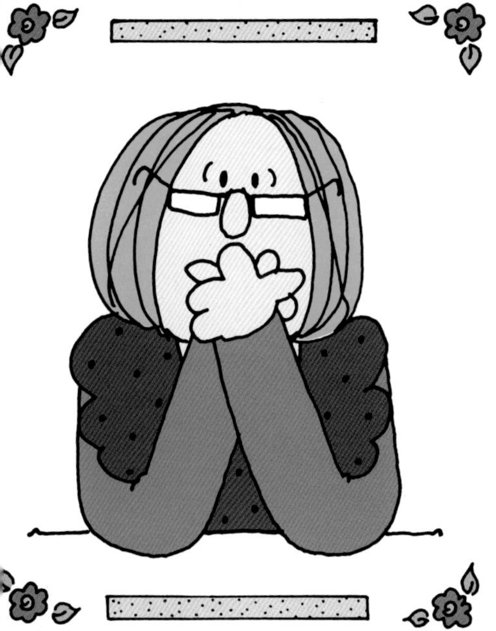

The family thigh
problem begins with
the mouth.

diet
diet
DONUTS

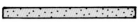

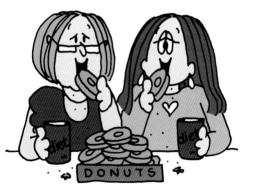

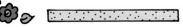

Verbal clippings:
All the aggravation, none
of the evidence.

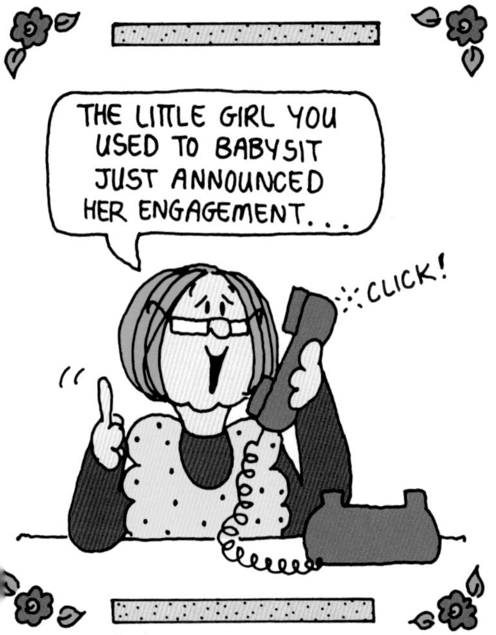
THE LITTLE GIRL YOU USED TO BABYSIT JUST ANNOUNCED HER ENGAGEMENT...
CLICK!

Some mothers
and daughters are
bonded. Some are
Crazy Glued.

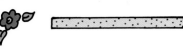

Competitive nurturing:
The final frontier.

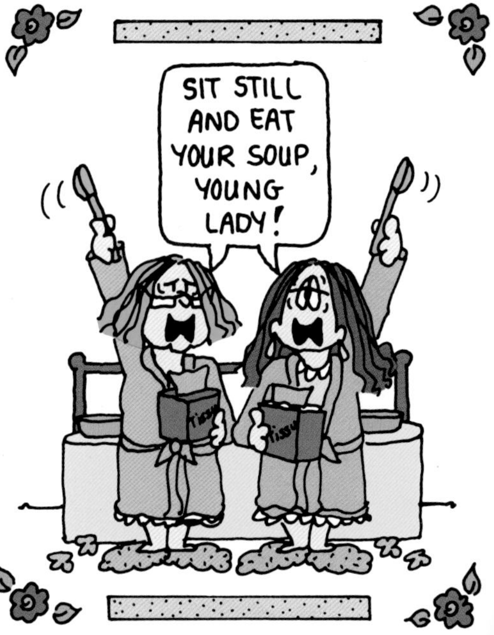
SIT STILL AND EAT YOUR SOUP, YOUNG LADY!
TISSUE
TISSUE

No matter where
you go or what you do,
your mother will always
be behind you . . . quietly
ripping her hair out.

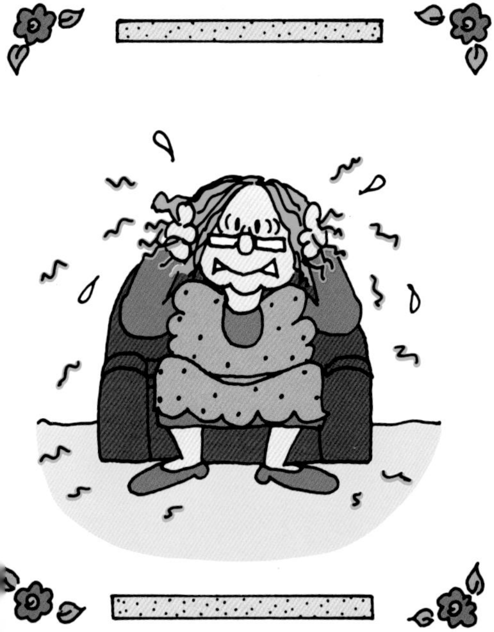

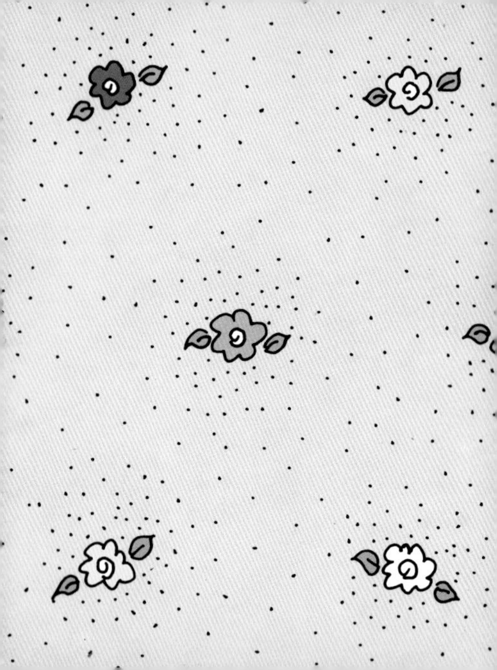